$14 In The Bank And A $200 Face In My Purse

Other Cathy® Books From Andrews and McMeel

My granddaughter has fleas!!
Why do the right words always come out of the wrong mouth?
A hand to hold, an opinion to reject
Thin thighs in thirty years
Wake me up when I'm a size 5
Men should come with instruction booklets
A mouthful of breath mints and no one to kiss
Another Saturday night of wild and reckless abandon

$14 In The Bank And A $200 Face In My Purse

A  Collection

 by Cathy Guisewite

Andrews and McMeel
A Universal Press Syndicate Company
Kansas City ▪ New York

ISBN: 0-8362-1820-5

Library of Congress Catalog Card Number: 90-82673

11

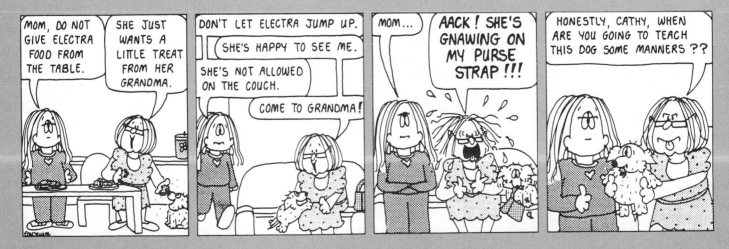

13

Panel 1: ONLY THREE WEEKS UNTIL SEPTEMBER AND I STILL HAVE TO GET ALL OF LITTLE BECKY'S SCHOOL OUTFITS READY!

Panel 2: ONLY THREE WEEKS LEFT AND BOB AND I STILL HAVE TO FINISH PAINTING THE DEN!

Panel 3: ONLY THREE WEEKS AND I STILL HAVE TO MEET SOMEONE, FALL IN LOVE, LOSE 10 POUNDS, BUY A TROPICAL ISLAND WARDROBE, GO ON A ROMANTIC SUMMER VACATION, GET MARRIED AND HAVE CHILDREN!

Panel 4: SAY WHAT YOU WILL ABOUT BUSY FAMILIES... SINGLE PEOPLE STILL HAVE MORE IMPRESSIVE LISTS.

Panel 5: THE LERNER MEMO! DOES ANYONE STILL HAVE A COPY OF THE LERNER MEMO?!

TA DA!

Panel 6: IT WAS BURIED UNDER THE HEAP OF EMERGENCIES DUE IN JULY, NEXT TO THE STACK OF CRISES STILL DUE FROM JUNE, ON TOP OF THE OVERNIGHT PACKAGES THAT CAME LAST WEEK THAT NO ONE HAS HAD TIME TO EVEN OPEN YET!!

Panel 7: BUT I FOUND IT!! TA DA!! I KNEW RIGHT WHERE IT WAS!!

Panel 8: IN A JOB LIKE THIS, WE LEARN TO CELEBRATE WHAT WE CAN....

Panel 9: THE FOOD IS WONDERFUL AND THE HOUSE IS LOVELY! I'M JUST GOING TO RUN TO THE POWDER ROOM AND FRESHEN UP.

RIGHT DOWN THE HALL.

Panel 11: AACK. BAM BAM STUFF WAD CRASH!

Panel 12: IF PEOPLE WANT THEIR PARTIES TO LAST PAST 8:00 P.M., THEY SHOULD LOCK UP THEIR SCALES.

18

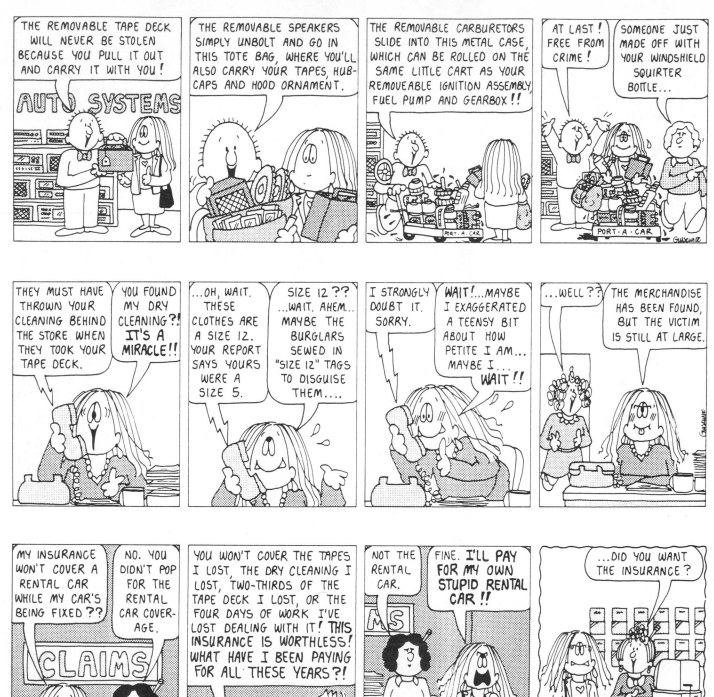

23

25

26

27

34

38

41

46

50

51

52

53

54

55

Panel 1: LET'S PLAY THE VIDEO FROM THIS MORNING! / REMEMBER WHEN IT USED TO TAKE **TWO WEEKS** TO GET THE CHRISTMAS MOVIES DEVELOPED??

Panel 2: HA, HA! REMEMBER WHEN IT TOOK **10 DAYS** TO GET THE CHRISTMAS PICTURES BACK?? / HA, HA!

Panel 3: READY? / click / **AACK!**

Panel 4: REMEMBER WHEN WE USED TO GET TO WAIT UNTIL AFTER NEW YEAR'S TO SEE HOW FAT WE WERE?

Panel 5: I'VE TYPED A LIST OF SUBJECTS I WON'T BRING UP DURING THE HOLIDAYS, CATHY. / A LIST?

Panel 6: ANY ONE OF THESE 46 SUBJECTS COULD ANNOY YOU AND RUIN YOUR VISIT. I WILL **NOT** BRING THEM UP!

Panel 7: MOTHER, DO YOU THINK I'M SO IMMATURE YOU HAVE TO HAVE A LIST OF TOPICS TO AVOID?! I CAN'T BELIEVE IT!!

Panel 8: #47: DO NOT MENTION THE LIST.

Panel 9: THE NEKERVISES ARE SPENDING CHRISTMAS WEEK TEACHING THEIR FIVE ADORABLE GRANDCHILDREN HOW TO FINGERPAINT LITTLE THANK-YOU NOTES...THE JOHNSTONS SPEND THE WEEK EDITING THEIR VIDEOS FROM LAST YEAR WITH A MEANINGFUL MUSICAL SOUNDTRACK...

Panel 10: FORTY-EIGHT HOURS AFTER CHRISTMAS, WE ARE STILL LYING AROUND IN GIFT WRAP RUBBLE, EATING FRUITCAKES I WAS SUPPOSED TO GIVE TO OTHER PEOPLE, BUT NEVER GOT AROUND TO SENDING....

Panel 11:

Panel 12: ...THEN AGAIN, I'LL TAKE ANY FAMILY TRADITION I CAN GET.

62

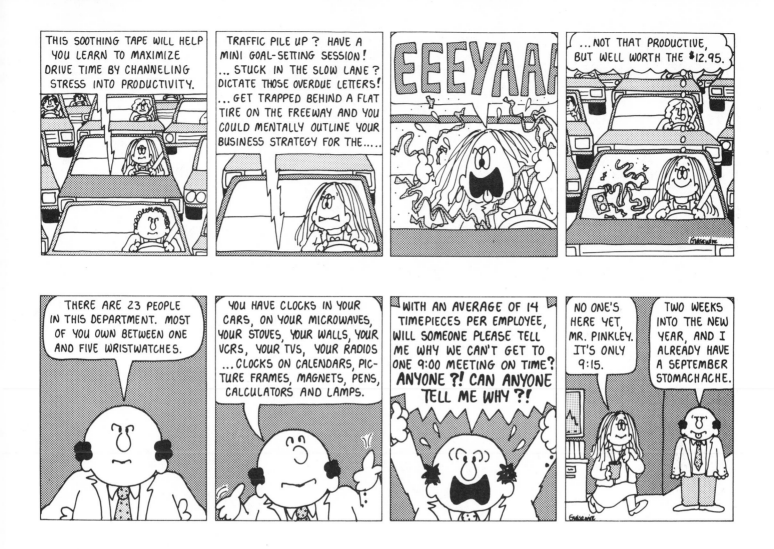

THIS SOOTHING TAPE WILL HELP YOU LEARN TO MAXIMIZE DRIVE TIME BY CHANNELING STRESS INTO PRODUCTIVITY.

TRAFFIC PILE UP ? HAVE A MINI GOAL-SETTING SESSION ! ... STUCK IN THE SLOW LANE ? DICTATE THOSE OVERDUE LETTERS ! ... GET TRAPPED BEHIND A FLAT TIRE ON THE FREEWAY AND YOU COULD MENTALLY OUTLINE YOUR BUSINESS STRATEGY FOR THE.....

EEEYAA!

... NOT THAT PRODUCTIVE, BUT WELL WORTH THE $12.95.

THERE ARE 23 PEOPLE IN THIS DEPARTMENT. MOST OF YOU OWN BETWEEN ONE AND FIVE WRISTWATCHES.

YOU HAVE CLOCKS IN YOUR CARS, ON YOUR MICROWAVES, YOUR STOVES, YOUR WALLS, YOUR VCRS, YOUR TVS, YOUR RADIOS ...CLOCKS ON CALENDARS, PICTURE FRAMES, MAGNETS, PENS, CALCULATORS AND LAMPS.

WITH AN AVERAGE OF 14 TIMEPIECES PER EMPLOYEE, WILL SOMEONE PLEASE TELL ME WHY WE CAN'T GET TO ONE 9:00 MEETING ON TIME ? ANYONE ?! CAN ANYONE TELL ME WHY ?!

NO ONE'S HERE YET, MR. PINKLEY. IT'S ONLY 9:15.

TWO WEEKS INTO THE NEW YEAR, AND I ALREADY HAVE A SEPTEMBER STOMACHACHE.

NO ONE REMEMBERED MY 2:30 MEETING ?

FRED IS STILL READING THE INSTRUCTION MANUAL FOR HIS 87-FUNCTION MINI APPOINTMENT COMPUTER.

SHELLEY IS STILL HUNTING FOR REFILLS THAT EXACTLY MATCH HER DATEBOOK COVER.

JEFF IS TRYING TO SWITCH FROM "DAY RUNNER" TO "FILO-FAX", BUT CAN'T DO IT UNTIL HE CAN BRIBE A SECRETARY TO REDO ALL HIS INDEX TABS...

WHAT'S WRONG WITH A PIECE OF PAPER AND A PENCIL ??

YOU HAVE NO GRASP OF TIME-MANAGEMENT, MR. PINKLEY.

69

70

71

72

75

79

83

84

Panel 1: JUST WHEN I'M STARTING TO FEEL PRETTY GOOD ABOUT MY-SELF FOR HAVING SURVIVED WINTER, THE SUMMER MAGA-ZINES ROLL OUT... HOT NEW SWIMWEAR... KICKY NEW HAIR-DOS... SLINKY LITTLE OUTFITS TO WEAR WHILE WHIPPING UP SEXY LITTLE DINNERS FOR TWO.

Panel 2: WHAT ARE THEY TRYING TO **DO** TO US ?? WHAT ARE THEY TRYING TO DO TO **ME** ?!!

Panel 4: AND WHERE CAN I GET THAT GOLD LAMÉ BUSTIER WITH MATCH-ING MINISKIRT ??

Panel 5: LOOK, CATHY, ON THIS NEW DIET YOU GET TO PICK...

NO. NO CHOICES. I WANT **ALL** CHOICES ELIMI-NATED FROM MY DIET.

Panel 6: FINE. JUST MAKE A LIST THAT ELIMINATES ALL YOUR CHOICES.

NO. I NEED **SOMEONE ELSE** TO ELIMINATE MY CHOICES FOR ME.

Panel 7: FINE. I'LL MAKE A LIST...

NO. I NEED TO **PAY** SOMEONE. IT WILL ONLY WORK IF I PAY A STRANGER A FORTUNE TO ELIMI-NATE EACH AND EVERY CHOICE !!

Panel 8: WELCOME TO AMERICA: LAND OF THE FREE, HOME OF THE BERSERK.

Panel 9: WHAT ARE THOSE, CATHY ?

I'M NOT SURE.

Panel 10: I THINK THEY TOOK ALL THE DIET BOOKS THAT DIDN'T WORK, GROUND THEM INTO A PULP, SMASHED THEM INTO LITTLE CRACKER SHAPES AND THEN BAKED THEM UNTIL THEY TURNED TO ROCK. ONLY 10 CALORIES EACH.

Panel 11: HM! NOT BAD!

BLEAH! THIS TASTES LIKE CARD-BOARD! HOW CAN YOU **LIKE** THIS?! BLEAH!!

Panel 12: THREE WEEKS BEFORE BATHING SUIT SEASON, IT ONLY HAS TO BE EDIBLE.

Panel 1: MY LIFE IS HALF OVER AND WHAT DO I HAVE TO SHOW FOR IT? NOTHING!

Panel 2: I'VE BEEN NOWHERE, ACCOMPLISHED NOTHING... MY BODY IS DETERIORATING, AND MY HAIR IS FALLING OUT.

Panel 3: I'M A WORTHLESS, WASTED, BALDING, HALF-BLIND BLOB OF UNUSED POTENTIAL!

Panel 4: ...NOW HE NEEDS ME.

Panel 5: THE AGING MAN HAS A ONE-IN-FIVE CHANCE OF HAVING A HEART ATTACK... ONE-IN-FIVE CHANCE OF KIDNEY STONES... THREE-IN-FIVE CHANCE OF PROSTATE TROUBLE...

Panel 6: ...AND A 99.9 PERCENT CHANCE OF WEAKER MUSCLES, POORER VISION, STIFFER JOINTS, REDUCED HEARING, LOWER SEX DRIVE AND.....

Panel 7: IRVING, YOU'RE YOUNG, HEALTHY AND STRONG! WHY ARE YOU THINKING LIKE THIS??

Panel 8: AACK! MY BRAIN HAS ALREADY STARTED TO SHRINK!!

Panel 9: HAVE SOME BIRTHDAY CAKE, IRVING. / TOO MUCH FAT. TOO MUCH CHOLESTEROL.

Panel 10: HEART DISEASE IS THE NO.1 KILLER OF MEN! WHAT ARE YOU TRYING TO DO?? **MURDER ME?!**

Panel 11: ~GLOMP~

Panel 12: THERE, NOW, DON'T YOU FEEL BETTER? / I HAVE TO GO FLOSS! I FEEL MY GUMS STARTING TO ROT!

Happy Birthday

110

113

115

118

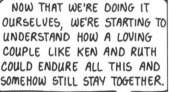